Introduction

Dear Parent and Child/Children!

Thank you for choosing My Cat Trevor.
I hope you enjoy reading the story together and looking
at the pictures to see what you can find!

One of my fondest memories as a child was to listen to
the sound of my Grandma's soothing voice as she gently
and lovingly read me to sleep, what a special memory to
cherish - I hope this book helps you to create a beautiful
memory that you can keep in your heart forever too.

As a mother I read to my Daughters gently and lovingly
while the sound of my soothing voice read them to sleep.
Our children grow up too quickly, I hope you enjoy
the time you have to read with your children and
treasure the memories you create together...

Enjoy the reading time you are about to begin together!

During your reading...

Dear Parent and Child/Children!

During your reading look out for the hidden
bees, rats and cows on some pages,
their sneaky and their cheeky so keep your
eyes open wide and see how many
you are able to find!

You can find:

 **10 BEES**    **10 COWS**   **10 RATS**

Hint: Be sure to check every nook and cranny!

**Have fun counting bees, rats
and cows that don't meow!**

My cat Trevor
has lost his meow.

I don't know how
he lost his meow.

Do you?

Trevor and I looked under the bed.

No meow under there.

We looked in
the wardrobe.

No meow in there.

What will Trevor do if he can't find his meow?

We could borrow a cow but that won't help him meow!

Trevor and I looked in the bin.

Not a meow to be found!

We checked the fireplace.

Not a meow in sight!

What will Trevor do
if he can't meow?

We could borrow a rat
but he won't sound like a cat!

Trevor and I looked in the shed.

No meow could we hear.

We looked in the garden.

Not a meow could be heard,
or even a bird.

Trevor does not wish
to sound like a cow!

Trevor does not wish
to sound like a rat!

Just when Trevor and I
were about to give up...

All of a sudden I heard a...

It did not sound like
a rat or a cow.

My cat Trevor had not lost his meow.

He did not wish to sound like a rat or a cow!

Printed in Great Britain
by Amazon